THE ROBOTIC TABLE TENNIS PLAYER

How Google DeepMind is Bridging the
Virtual and Physical Worlds of AI

Alejandro S. Diego

Table of Contents

Introduction

In the vast expanse of technological innovation, there are moments that redefine the boundaries of what machines can achieve. The advent of artificial intelligence has been one such frontier, but the recent developments in robotics have pushed these boundaries even further. Picture a world where a machine not only learns but competes, where the line between human skill and artificial precision begins to blur. This is not a distant future—it's happening now, and it's happening in a way that challenges our very understanding of what robots are capable of.

At the heart of this revolution is Google DeepMind, a name synonymous with groundbreaking AI research. Their latest creation, a robot trained to play table tennis against humans, stands as a testament to the extraordinary leap from theoretical simulations to real-world performance. This is no ordinary robot. It's a symbol of how far we've come in the journey to merge the digital and physical worlds, and it marks a new chapter in the history of AI.

Table tennis, a sport known for its lightning-fast reflexes and intricate strategies, has long been a domain where human skill reigns supreme. Yet, here we have a machine not just participating but competing, pushing back against the very limitations we once thought were insurmountable for AI. The creation of this robotic player represents more than just a technical achievement; it signals the dawn of a new era where robots are no longer confined to controlled environments but are stepping into our world, learning, adapting, and evolving.

The significance of this breakthrough cannot be overstated. It's a milestone that showcases the incredible potential of AI to perform tasks that require a high degree of precision and adaptability. More importantly, it opens up a world of possibilities where the virtual simulations that train these machines become indistinguishable from the real-life challenges they are designed to overcome. This bridging of the gap between the digital and the physical is the key to unlocking the full potential of robotics in the real world.

As we embark on this journey through the story of Google DeepMind's table tennis robot, you'll discover not just the technology behind the machine but the broader implications it holds for the future. This is a story of innovation, challenge, and the relentless pursuit of excellence that is reshaping our world in ways we are only beginning to understand. The pages ahead will delve into the fascinating process that brought this robot to life, the hurdles it overcame, and the visionaries who made it possible. Prepare yourself for a tale that will not only inform but inspire, as we explore the future of robotics and the new horizons it promises to unveil.

Chapter 1: The Evolution of AI in Sports

Artificial intelligence has long captivated our imagination, especially in the realm of games, where the intellectual prowess of machines has been pitted against the best human minds. The journey of AI in competitive gaming began with classic board games like Chess, where IBM's Deep Blue famously defeated world champion Garry Kasparov in 1997. This victory was more than just a headline—it was a turning point, demonstrating that AI could not only compete with but surpass human expertise in complex, strategic thinking.

From Chess, the field of AI moved on to even more challenging games, each presenting unique hurdles. Google's DeepMind made waves with its AI program, AlphaGo, which conquered the ancient Chinese board game Go in 2016 by defeating Lee Sedol, one of the world's top players. Go, with its near-infinite number of possible moves, was considered far more complex than Chess, and AlphaGo's victory was seen as a monumental achievement in AI. It was here that the true potential of AI began to crystallize, showing that machines could not only analyze but also anticipate and innovate in ways that were previously thought to be the exclusive domain of human intuition.

The success didn't stop there. DeepMind continued to push the boundaries, venturing into the world of real-time strategy games like Starcraft II. Unlike Chess and Go, Starcraft II requires players to make decisions in real-time, managing resources, building armies, and outmaneuvering opponents with speed and precision. AlphaStar, DeepMind's AI for Starcraft II, demonstrated that AI could master the complexity of dynamic environments, where strategy must be constantly adapted to changing conditions. This was a new level of achievement, showcasing AI's ability to operate effectively in environments that mimic real-world scenarios.

With these successes under its belt, DeepMind set its sights on a new frontier: the physical world of sports. Unlike the digital confines of Chess, Go, or Starcraft, sports involve not just strategic thinking but physical execution, a domain where machines have traditionally struggled. The transition from mastering games played on a board or a screen to excelling in a sport like table tennis represents a significant leap. It's not just about understanding the game's rules or strategies; it's about embodying them in a physical form, responding to the unpredictable nature of human opponents in real-time.

Google DeepMind's history with AI-driven games laid the foundation for this next step. Each success in the digital realm provided valuable insights and technologies that could be adapted and expanded upon for use in the physical world. The challenge now was to take the advanced algorithms that had dominated Chess, Go, and Starcraft and translate them into a machine capable of competing on a real-world playing field. This is where the story of the robotic table tennis player begins—a tale of translating digital mastery into physical reality, of taking on the ultimate test of AI: not just to think like a human, but to act like one too.

Choosing table tennis as the arena for advancing AI into the physical realm was no arbitrary decision. Table tennis is a sport that demands a combination of rapid reflexes, precise movements, and strategic thinking—all executed in real-time. It's a game where the margin for error is incredibly slim, and every fraction of a second counts. For these reasons, table tennis presents a unique and formidable challenge for AI, pushing the boundaries of what machines can do when faced with the unpredictability and speed of a human opponent.

The challenges of applying AI to a sport like table tennis are manifold. Unlike board games, where decisions are made based on a static environment, table tennis involves a constantly changing physical space. The ball's speed, spin, and trajectory can vary wildly from one moment to the next, requiring the AI to process visual information, predict outcomes, and execute precise movements—all in the blink of an eye. This requires a level of coordination and adaptability that far exceeds the demands of purely strategic games.

Moreover, table tennis is not just about reacting; it's about anticipating. A skilled human player uses deception, varying their shots to confuse and outmaneuver their opponent. For an AI, understanding and responding to these subtleties in real-time is a monumental task. It's not enough to simply return the ball; the AI must understand the nuances of the game—how to adjust its strategy based on the opponent's style, how to deal with unexpected spins, and how to maintain a rhythm in the face of relentless, rapid exchanges.

Yet, with these challenges come significant opportunities. The successful application of AI in table tennis represents a breakthrough in robotics and AI, showcasing the ability to translate complex digital algorithms into physical actions. It's a demonstration of how far AI has come in its ability to interact with the physical world in a meaningful way. The skills learned in mastering table tennis—speed, precision, adaptability—are directly transferable to a wide range of other tasks, from industrial automation to advanced robotics in healthcare and home assistance.

The significance of this achievement extends far beyond the sport itself. In the broader context of AI and robotics, mastering table tennis is a symbolic victory. It represents a crucial step in the journey towards creating robots that can function autonomously in dynamic, real-world environments. This isn't just about winning games; it's about developing the foundational technologies that will enable robots to work alongside humans, in settings that require both physical dexterity and cognitive flexibility.

In many ways, table tennis is the perfect testbed for these technologies. It's a sport that encapsulates the unpredictability and complexity of the real world, offering a microcosm where AI can be pushed to its limits. By taking on such a challenging and fast-paced sport, Google DeepMind has shown that AI is capable of not just understanding the physical world, but thriving within it. This achievement marks a pivotal moment in the evolution of AI, one that brings us closer to a future where robots are not just tools, but active participants in the world we live in.

Chapter 2: From Simulation to Reality

In the world of robotics, the journey from virtual simulations to real-world applications is far from straightforward. This transition is often referred to as the "Sim-to-Real Gap," a concept that underscores one of the most significant challenges in robotics and AI development. At its core, the Sim-to-Real Gap highlights the differences between training a robot in a controlled, simulated environment and having that robot perform effectively in the unpredictable and complex physical world.

Simulations provide a safe and efficient way to teach robots the basics. In a virtual environment, parameters can be controlled, and countless scenarios can be generated without the wear and tear on physical components. For instance, in a simulation, a robot can play thousands of table tennis matches in a fraction of the time it would take in the real world, learning the mechanics of the game—how to hit a forehand, return a serve, or position itself on the table. However, the challenges arise when these learned skills must be transferred from the virtual world to the real one.

The real world is full of variables that are difficult to replicate in a simulation. Factors like lighting, temperature, material properties, and even minor imperfections in the physical setup can significantly impact a robot's performance. A table tennis ball, for example, might behave slightly differently on a real table than in a simulation due to surface texture or environmental conditions. Moreover, the physical robot must deal with the limitations of its hardware—motors, sensors, and joints that may not perform with the same precision and speed as their simulated counterparts.

One of the primary challenges in bridging the Sim-to-Real Gap is ensuring that the robot's virtual training translates accurately to its physical actions. In simulations, the robot can be equipped with perfect sensors and limitless processing power, but in reality, it must rely on actual hardware, which comes with its own set of limitations. Sensors might be less accurate, motors might not respond as quickly, and physical wear and tear can introduce inconsistencies over time.

To overcome these challenges, researchers at Google DeepMind employed a process of iterative refinement. The robot was initially trained in a simulation to develop its basic skills, but this was only the first step. The real breakthrough came when these virtual skills were tested and fine-tuned in the physical world. By continuously adjusting and improving the robot's performance based on real-world data, the researchers were able to gradually close the gap between simulation and reality.

This process of iterative learning is crucial because it allows the robot to adapt to the nuances of the real world that are impossible to fully capture in a simulation. Each time the robot played a real game of table tennis, it encountered new variables—subtle changes in the way the ball moved, differences in human opponents' playing styles, or even slight variations in the environment. By incorporating these real-world experiences back into its learning process, the robot could refine its skills and improve its performance in ways that pure simulation could never achieve.

Understanding and overcoming the Sim-to-Real Gap is not just a technical achievement; it's a fundamental step towards creating robots that can operate autonomously in the real world. The ability to transfer virtual skills into physical actions opens the door to a wide range of applications, from autonomous vehicles navigating unpredictable environments to robotic assistants that can safely interact with humans in complex settings. The work done by Google DeepMind in this area is not just about teaching a robot to play table tennis; it's about pioneering the techniques that will allow AI to transition from the lab to the real world, where it can have a tangible impact on our daily lives.

The process of training a robot to play table tennis at a competitive level is a complex and meticulous endeavor, requiring a careful blend of simulation-based learning and real-world refinement. This two-step training process is designed to harness the best of both worlds—leveraging the efficiency and control of virtual environments while grounding the robot's skills in the unpredictability of real-life interactions.

The journey begins in the simulated world, where the robot is introduced to the fundamental mechanics of table tennis. This initial phase is crucial, as it allows the robot to learn the basics—how to position itself, how to move its paddle, and how to respond to various types of shots. The use of Mujoco, an advanced physics engine, plays a pivotal role in this stage. Mujoco enables the simulation of complex physical interactions with a high degree of accuracy, allowing the robot to practice in a virtual environment that closely mimics the real world.

In Mujoco, the robot can undergo countless iterations of practice, trying different techniques and strategies without the physical constraints or risks of real-world training. This is where it learns to perform essential table tennis skills, such as executing forehand and backhand shots, handling spin, and maintaining a rally. The beauty of this approach is that it accelerates the learning process—what might take months or even years of real-world practice can be compressed into a much shorter timeframe in the virtual world.

However, mastering the game in a simulation is only half the battle. The transition from virtual perfection to real-world competency is fraught with challenges, many of which stem from the inherent differences between a controlled simulation and the chaotic nature of reality. This is where the second step of the training process—real-world fine-tuning—comes into play.

Once the robot has achieved a certain level of proficiency in the simulation, it is introduced to the physical world. Here, it faces real opponents, real tables, and real balls—each with their own quirks and variations that were not present in the virtual environment. The robot's interactions with human players are particularly valuable during this phase, as they expose it to a wide range of playing styles and techniques that are difficult to replicate in a simulation.

The fine-tuning process is iterative by nature. Initially, the robot may struggle with certain aspects of the game, such as adjusting to the varying speeds and spins applied by human opponents or dealing with the subtle inconsistencies in real-world conditions. Each time the robot plays a match, the data collected from its performance is fed back into its learning system. This data includes everything from the trajectory of the ball to the timing of the opponent's shots, all of which are used to refine the robot's strategies and improve its physical responses.

One of the major obstacles in this phase is the lack of initial data. Since robots playing table tennis against humans is a relatively new concept, there was no vast library of data to draw from at the outset. The researchers had to build this dataset from scratch, collecting information during each real-world match and using it to continuously update the robot's capabilities. This iterative approach—where the robot's performance is constantly evaluated and refined—was critical in helping it overcome the challenges posed by the transition from simulation to reality.

Through repeated cycles of real-world interaction and refinement, the robot gradually improved its ability to compete at a human level. It learned to anticipate its opponent's moves more accurately, to adjust its strategy on the fly, and to execute its shots with greater precision. The fine-tuning process not only enhanced the robot's technical skills but also helped it adapt to the unpredictable elements of real-world gameplay, such as changes in lighting, minor imperfections in the playing surface, and the varying skill levels of human players.

This two-step training process, combining the controlled efficiency of simulation with the adaptive learning of real-world experience, represents a significant advancement in the field of robotics. It demonstrates how AI can be trained to perform complex physical tasks that require both precision and flexibility—skills that are essential for robots to operate effectively in dynamic, real-world environments. The success of this approach with the table tennis robot opens up new possibilities for applying similar techniques to a wide range of other robotic applications, from manufacturing to healthcare, where the ability to learn and adapt is crucial.

Chapter 3: The Robotic Player in Action

When pitting the robot against human players in 29 matches, the results were a compelling mix of triumph and learning opportunities. Out of these matches, the robot managed to secure victory in 13, a notable achievement given the complexities of the game and the varying skill levels of the human opponents. This performance not only highlighted the robot's capabilities but also provided valuable insights into where it excelled and where it still had room for improvement.

One of the robot's primary strengths lay in its consistency and precision. In the realm of speed and accuracy, it often outperformed human players, particularly in scenarios that required quick reflexes. The robot's ability to track the ball's movement with cameras and process this information almost instantaneously allowed it to react faster than many of its human counterparts. This speed was especially evident in rallies, where the robot could maintain a steady pace, returning shots with a level of accuracy that humans found challenging to counter consistently.

However, the robot's proficiency wasn't without its limitations. While it excelled in straightforward rallies and could handle a variety of standard shots with ease, it struggled with more advanced techniques, particularly when dealing with spin. Spin is a critical element in table tennis, used by skilled players to control the ball's trajectory and deceive their opponents. The robot, despite its advanced sensors and algorithms, found it difficult to accurately read and respond to the subtle variations in spin applied by more experienced players. This weakness occasionally left it vulnerable, especially when faced with rapid, heavily spun shots that required not just speed but nuanced adjustments in paddle angle and force.

Another area where the robot showed both promise and limitation was in strategic play. The robot's strategy was largely based on the vast amounts of data it had been fed during its training. It could analyze patterns, predict the opponent's next move, and position itself accordingly. In matches against less experienced players, this data-driven approach often gave the robot an edge, allowing it to anticipate and counter its opponent's tactics effectively. However, when playing against more advanced humans who could adapt their strategies on the fly, the robot sometimes lagged. It could become predictable, relying on patterns that more seasoned players could exploit.

These 29 matches served as a crucial testing ground, revealing not only the robot's technical prowess but also the areas where human intuition and adaptability still hold sway. The victories it secured were a testament to the progress made in robotics and AI, demonstrating that a machine could indeed compete with human players in a fast-paced, real-world sport. Yet, the losses were equally important, highlighting the complexities of the human game that AI has yet to fully master.

The robot's performance in these matches underscores the dual nature of AI's progress: remarkable in its ability to replicate human-like precision and speed, but still grappling with the more nuanced aspects of human strategy and creativity. Each match provided invaluable feedback, informing future iterations of the robot's design and programming. The strengths it displayed in speed and consistency are clear indicators of how far AI has come, while its struggles with spin and strategy remind us that the journey is ongoing, with many challenges still to be conquered.

In summary, the robot's performance against human opponents was a blend of impressive successes and revealing shortcomings. Its victories demonstrated the power of AI in mastering the technical aspects of a complex sport, while its losses highlighted the areas where human ingenuity remains a formidable challenge. As the technology continues to evolve, these insights will be crucial in refining the robot's abilities, bringing it ever closer to not just competing with, but potentially surpassing, human skill in the game of table tennis.

When humans step into the role of playing against a machine, the experience is often met with a mixture of curiosity, excitement, and a touch of apprehension. In the case of the table tennis robot developed by Google DeepMind, this interaction was no different. Human players, ranging from novices to seasoned enthusiasts, found themselves facing off against a machine that was not just fast and precise but also capable of learning and adapting in real time. This novel experience offered a glimpse into the future of human-robot interaction, raising intriguing questions about the role of AI in our lives.

The reactions from human players were diverse but largely positive. For many, the opportunity to play against a robot was an exciting and unique challenge. The robot's ability to consistently return shots, maintain rallies, and even outmaneuver some opponents made the matches engaging and, at times, exhilarating. Players were often surprised by how quickly the robot could react to their moves, which added an element of unpredictability to the game. This unpredictability, coupled with the robot's consistent performance, kept players on their toes, making the experience both challenging and enjoyable.

However, the human element in this interaction was not lost. Despite its advanced capabilities, the robot was designed with the goal of creating an enjoyable and engaging experience for its human counterparts. The developers understood that for the robot to be more than just a technical novelty, it needed to offer a game that was not only competitive but also fun. This focus on enjoyment was critical, as it ensured that players felt motivated to continue playing, rather than being frustrated by an unbeatable machine.

Player feedback played a crucial role in refining the robot's design and performance. After each match, players were asked to rate their experience, providing insights into what worked well and what could be improved. Many players appreciated the robot's consistency and speed, noting that it provided a good workout and a chance to improve their own skills. However, some also pointed out areas where the robot could improve, such as its ability to handle complex spins or its occasional predictability in strategy.

This feedback was invaluable to the developers at DeepMind. By listening to the players' experiences, they were able to make adjustments that enhanced the robot's ability to deliver a more balanced and enjoyable game. For example, when players reported that the robot's predictability made the game less challenging over time, the developers worked on introducing more variability in the robot's responses, making it harder to anticipate and thus more engaging to play against.

The impact of this player feedback extended beyond just improving the robot's performance. It also highlighted the importance of human-centered design in robotics. The developers recognized that for AI to truly integrate into activities like sports, it needs to be responsive not just in a technical sense but also in a way that resonates with human emotions and expectations. The robot had to be more than just a competitor; it needed to be a partner in the game, one that could push players to improve while also making the experience enjoyable.

This focus on human interaction also provided valuable lessons for future developments in robotics. As robots become more integrated into our daily lives, whether in sports, work, or home environments, their ability to engage with humans in a meaningful and enjoyable way will be critical to their success. The table tennis robot served as a testing ground for these principles, demonstrating that when robots are designed with the human experience in mind, they can offer not just efficiency and precision but also a sense of fun and challenge that enhances the overall interaction.

In conclusion, the human players who faced off against the table tennis robot experienced more than just a game; they engaged with a new kind of opponent, one that pushed the boundaries of what machines can do. Their reactions, both positive and constructive, played a pivotal role in shaping the robot's development, ensuring that it was not only a technical marvel but also a participant in a shared experience. This emphasis on human-centered design will continue to guide the evolution of robotics, as we move toward a future where machines and humans play, work, and interact side by side.

Chapter 4: The Technology Behind the Scenes

Creating a robotic athlete capable of competing in a fast-paced and highly skilled sport like table tennis requires a sophisticated blend of hardware that can not only mimic human movements but also operate with the precision and speed necessary to excel in the game. At the core of this technological marvel are several key components that work together to bring the robot to life, each playing a crucial role in enabling it to perform at a competitive level.

One of the most critical components of the robot is its visual system, which is comprised of high-speed cameras. These cameras are the robot's eyes, constantly tracking the movement of the ball with remarkable accuracy. In table tennis, where the ball can travel at high speeds and change direction in an instant, the ability to capture and process visual information in real-time is essential. These cameras are linked to an advanced motion capture system that monitors not only the ball but also the movements of the human opponent. This system allows the robot to anticipate and react to its opponent's shots, adjusting its position and paddle angle with split-second precision.

The motion capture system plays another vital role in the robot's performance. By capturing the movements of the human player, the system provides the robot with critical data on the opponent's strategy and shot placement. This information is processed by the robot's onboard computers, which then calculate the best possible response. The integration of these systems ensures that the robot can keep up with the rapid pace of the game, making quick and accurate decisions that mirror the instincts of a human player.

Beyond the visual and motion capture systems, the physical construction of the robot is designed with careful consideration of the demands of table tennis. One of the key challenges in building this robotic athlete was replicating the physical properties of a table tennis paddle in the simulation environment. The paddle is not just a simple tool; its texture, weight, and flexibility all contribute to how the ball is hit, spun, and controlled. For the robot to effectively compete, it needed to wield a paddle that behaved in the same way a human's would.

In the simulation phase of training, the developers used the Mujoco physics engine to meticulously model the paddle's characteristics. They considered factors such as the softness of the rubber surface, the stiffness of the paddle, and the way it interacts with the ball upon contact. This level of detail was crucial because even small differences in these physical properties could significantly affect the robot's ability to control the ball. By ensuring that the virtual paddle in the simulation behaved exactly like a real one, the developers were able to provide the robot with a realistic training experience that could be seamlessly transferred to the physical world.

When it came time to build the robot's physical paddle, the same attention to detail was applied. The paddle was constructed to match the exact specifications used in the simulation, from the materials used to the way it was mounted on the robot's arm. This replication was vital for maintaining the continuity between the robot's simulated training and its real-world performance. It allowed the robot to apply the skills and strategies it had learned in the simulation directly to the physical game, without the need to adjust for differences in equipment.

The robot's arm, which holds and maneuvers the paddle, was also a critical focus of the design. It needed to be both strong and agile, capable of moving swiftly to intercept the ball and applying the precise amount of force required to return it accurately. The developers engineered the arm with advanced servomotors that provided the necessary speed and torque, while also incorporating sensors that gave the robot feedback on the position and movement of its arm in real-time. This setup allowed the robot to make fine adjustments during the game, ensuring that its shots were as accurate and controlled as possible.

Together, these hardware components form the foundation of the robotic athlete, enabling it to compete in a sport that demands both physical dexterity and cognitive skill. The integration of high-speed cameras, motion capture systems, and carefully engineered physical components creates a robot that not only moves like a human but also thinks and reacts in ways that are eerily human-like. This combination of cutting-edge technology and meticulous design underscores the complexity and innovation involved in building a robot capable of playing table tennis at a competitive level.

The success of this robot in real-world matches is a testament to the importance of hardware in AI development. While advanced algorithms and learning models are essential, the physical components that bring these digital processes into the real world are equally crucial. By focusing on the precise replication of human tools and movements, the developers of this robotic athlete have taken a significant step toward bridging the gap between AI and human ability, demonstrating that with the right technology, robots can indeed hold their own in the physical world.

While the hardware provides the physical foundation for the robotic table tennis player, it is the software—the AI algorithms at play—that truly animates the machine, allowing it to compete in a game as dynamic and complex as table tennis. The interplay between low-level and high-level controllers within the AI system is what enables the robot to perform with such remarkable precision, adaptability, and strategic insight.

At the core of the robot's functionality are the low-level controllers. These controllers are responsible for executing the fundamental actions that the robot performs during a match. Think of these as the basic building blocks of its gameplay—everything from moving the paddle to striking the ball with the correct force and angle. The low-level controllers handle the fine motor skills required to play table tennis, managing the exact positioning of the paddle, the timing of swings, and the precise adjustments needed to return the ball accurately.

These low-level controllers were developed through extensive training in simulated environments, where the robot learned the mechanics of the game. By practicing thousands of repetitions of specific shots—forehand smashes, backhand returns, and even complex spins—the AI was able to develop a "library" of skills that could be called upon during a match. Each of these skills is finely tuned, allowing the robot to perform actions with a level of consistency and precision that rivals, and in some cases exceeds, that of human players.

However, low-level control alone is not enough to succeed in a game like table tennis, where strategy and adaptability play crucial roles. This is where the high-level controllers come into play. The high-level controllers are responsible for making strategic decisions during the match. They analyze the current state of play—considering factors such as the opponent's position, the spin on the ball, and the potential trajectories—and decide on the best course of action.

These decisions are made in real-time, as the robot processes data from its sensors and anticipates the next move. For example, if the opponent applies a heavy topspin, the high-level controller will determine whether the robot should counter with a defensive block or attempt a more aggressive shot. The controller takes into account not only the immediate situation but also the broader context of the match, such as the score, the opponent's tendencies, and the overall pace of the game.

One of the most impressive aspects of the robot's AI is its ability to adapt to new opponents and unpredictable gameplay scenarios. This adaptability is a result of the AI's underlying algorithms, which are designed to learn from experience and refine their strategies over time. When the robot encounters an unfamiliar opponent, it doesn't rely solely on pre-programmed responses; instead, it analyzes the opponent's style, identifies patterns, and adjusts its gameplay accordingly.

For instance, if a new opponent frequently uses fast, low shots, the AI will recognize this pattern after a few exchanges and begin positioning the robot to better counter these types of shots. Similarly, if the opponent tends to favor a particular side of the table, the AI can shift its strategy to exploit this tendency, perhaps by forcing the opponent to play on their weaker side.

This level of adaptability is achieved through a combination of machine learning techniques and real-time data processing. As the robot plays more matches, it continues to refine its understanding of different playing styles and strategies, incorporating this knowledge into its high-level decision-making process. This continuous learning loop allows the AI to become increasingly sophisticated in its gameplay, making it a formidable opponent even for experienced human players.

The robot's ability to handle unpredictable scenarios is another key feature of its software design. Table tennis is a sport full of surprises—unusual spins, unexpected bounces, and deceptive moves are all part of the game. The AI must be able to respond to these surprises without missing a beat. To achieve this, the software is designed to be flexible and responsive, with the high-level controllers capable of making quick adjustments based on new information. Whether it's a sudden change in the ball's trajectory or a surprising move from the opponent, the AI can rapidly recalibrate its strategy and continue to play effectively.

This dual-layered approach, with low-level controllers handling the execution of specific actions and high-level controllers managing overall strategy, is what makes the robot such a capable and adaptive player. The combination of precise control and strategic intelligence allows the robot to not only compete but to continuously improve, learning from each match and refining its approach to the game.

In conclusion, the software driving the robotic table tennis player is a complex interplay of algorithms that enable both fine motor control and strategic adaptability. The low-level controllers ensure the robot can perform the physical actions needed to play the game, while the high-level controllers allow it to think strategically, adapt to new opponents, and handle unpredictable scenarios. Together, these elements create a robotic athlete that is not just a marvel of engineering but a true competitor in the sport, capable of pushing the boundaries of what AI can achieve in the physical world.

Chapter 5: Challenges and Limitations

Despite the impressive capabilities of the robotic table tennis player, there are still areas where it falls short, revealing the ongoing challenges in developing AI that can fully replicate human dexterity and adaptability. These limitations are important to consider, not just as technical obstacles, but as reminders of the complexity of human skills and the nuanced understanding required to master them.

One of the most significant challenges the robot faces is dealing with extreme spins and fast balls. Spin is a fundamental aspect of table tennis, used by skilled players to control the trajectory and behavior of the ball in ways that can be difficult to predict and counter. While the robot is adept at handling standard shots and even moderate spins, it struggles with the more advanced spins that experienced players use to deceive and outmaneuver their opponents. The robot's sensors and algorithms, although highly sophisticated, are not yet capable of fully capturing and interpreting the subtle variations in spin that can drastically alter the ball's path.

For instance, when an opponent applies a heavy topspin or backspin, the ball might dip or rise unexpectedly, requiring quick adjustments in paddle angle and timing to return the shot effectively. While the robot can recognize and react to these changes to some extent, it often lacks the fine-tuned sensitivity needed to counter such spins consistently. This limitation becomes particularly evident in matches against higher-level players who use spin as a strategic weapon, exploiting the robot's difficulty in adapting to these rapid changes.

Another area where the robot's performance is limited is in its ability to handle extremely fast balls. In high-speed rallies, where the ball is traveling at velocities that push the limits of human reaction time, the robot's response can sometimes lag. Although its cameras and motion capture systems are designed to track the ball with great precision, the sheer speed of the ball in these situations can overwhelm the processing capabilities of the AI, leading to mistimed swings or missed opportunities. This is particularly challenging when the ball is hit with a combination of speed and spin, creating a scenario that tests the limits of both the robot's hardware and software.

Perhaps the most conspicuous limitation of the robot is its inability to serve the ball. Serving in table tennis is not just about getting the ball into play; it's a critical component of strategy, allowing the server to dictate the pace and spin of the game from the outset. The serve is often a carefully crafted move, with players using a variety of spins, speeds, and placements to gain an advantage. Unfortunately, the robot has not yet been equipped with the capability to perform this essential part of the game. This limitation is due to the complex coordination required to deliver a serve that is not only legal according to the rules of the game but also strategic in nature.

To accommodate this inability, the developers have had to make modifications to the standard rules of table tennis during matches involving the robot. In these matches, the human opponent serves every time, allowing the game to proceed without requiring the robot to initiate play. While this workaround enables the robot to participate in competitive matches, it also highlights a significant gap in its capabilities. The lack of a serving ability is not just a technical shortcoming; it limits the robot's strategic options and reduces its overall effectiveness as a competitor.

These limitations, while significant, are also areas of active research and development. The challenges of dealing with extreme spins, fast balls, and serving are not insurmountable, but they require further advancements in both the hardware and software that drive the robot. Improving the robot's ability to handle these aspects of the game will involve enhancing its sensory inputs, refining its processing algorithms, and possibly redesigning its mechanical components to allow for more nuanced and precise control.

In conclusion, the robotic table tennis player, despite its many strengths, still faces notable limitations that underscore the complexities of human skill in sports. The challenges of dealing with advanced spins, high-speed rallies, and the inability to serve highlight the areas where AI and robotics still have room to grow. These shortcomings serve as a reminder that while AI has made tremendous strides, replicating the full range of human abilities remains a formidable task. As research continues, overcoming these limitations will be crucial in advancing the capabilities of robots not only in table tennis but in a wide range of real-world applications.

The journey of developing a robotic table tennis player has been marked by remarkable achievements, but it has also illuminated several obstacles that must be overcome to push the boundaries of what AI and robotics can accomplish. As we look toward the future, the path forward involves addressing these challenges through advancements in predictive AI models, refining algorithms, and expanding the applications of these technologies beyond the confines of sports.

One of the most promising avenues for overcoming the robot's current limitations lies in the development of more advanced predictive AI models. These models would enable the robot to anticipate an opponent's moves with greater accuracy, allowing it to react not just to what is happening in the moment but also to what is likely to happen next. By incorporating more sophisticated pattern recognition and machine learning techniques, the AI could begin to "read" the game in the way a skilled human player does, predicting shots based on subtle cues in the opponent's body language, positioning, and previous actions.

For example, a more advanced predictive model could help the robot better handle extreme spins and fast balls by not only reacting to the ball's immediate movement but also anticipating the spin's effect before the ball reaches it. This would give the robot a critical edge in high-speed rallies, where the margin for error is razor-thin. Additionally, enhancing the robot's ability to predict the outcome of a shot could improve its strategic play, allowing it to set up more effective counterattacks and to exploit the weaknesses of its opponent more effectively.

Alongside improvements in predictive modeling, better algorithms will play a key role in advancing the robot's capabilities. Current algorithms, while highly sophisticated, still have limitations when it comes to handling the full range of variables present in a real-world game of table tennis. By refining these algorithms, developers can create AI systems that are more adaptable and resilient, capable of adjusting to new and unexpected situations with greater ease.

One area of focus will be on developing algorithms that can more effectively manage the robot's decision-making process in real-time, especially when faced with complex and rapidly changing scenarios. These algorithms would allow the robot to process and prioritize multiple streams of data simultaneously—such as the ball's trajectory, the opponent's position, and the spin on the ball—enabling it to make split-second decisions that are both accurate and strategic.

Another promising development is the potential for integrating AI with more advanced robotics hardware, particularly in the area of sensory inputs and motor control. As sensors become more sensitive and motors more precise, the robot's physical capabilities will likely improve, allowing it to perform actions that were previously beyond its reach, such as executing a legal and strategic serve. By combining these hardware advancements with improved software, the next generation of robotic athletes could be even more lifelike in their movements and decision-making processes.

Looking beyond the realm of sports, the advancements made in developing this robotic table tennis player have far-reaching implications for AI in other real-world applications. The challenges of dealing with unpredictability, making real-time decisions, and interacting with human beings are not unique to table tennis; they are relevant to many fields, from autonomous vehicles to healthcare robots.

For instance, the same predictive models and algorithms that help the robot anticipate a table tennis opponent's moves could be adapted to improve the safety and efficiency of self-driving cars, allowing them to predict and respond to the behavior of other drivers and pedestrians with greater accuracy. Similarly, the fine motor control and adaptability developed for the robot could enhance the capabilities of surgical robots, enabling them to perform delicate procedures with a higher degree of precision and responsiveness.

In the industrial sector, robots equipped with these advanced AI systems could work more effectively alongside human workers, adapting to the dynamic conditions of a manufacturing environment or assisting in tasks that require both strength and dexterity. The lessons learned from the table tennis robot's development could lead to more intelligent, autonomous machines that are capable of operating safely and efficiently in a wide range of settings.

As AI continues to evolve, the boundaries between what is possible and what is still out of reach will continue to shift. The robotic table tennis player is just one example of how AI can be applied to complex, real-world challenges, but it represents a broader trend towards increasingly capable and autonomous machines. The path forward will involve not only refining the technologies that already exist but also exploring new possibilities that have yet to be imagined.

In conclusion, the future of AI in sports and beyond is full of potential, driven by advancements in predictive modeling, algorithm refinement, and the integration of smarter, more responsive hardware. While the road ahead is challenging, each step forward brings us closer to a world where AI and robotics are not just tools but true collaborators, capable of enhancing human abilities and transforming how we live, work, and play.

Chapter 6: The Broader Implications of AI in Robotics

The development of a robotic table tennis player by Google DeepMind is more than just a technical achievement; it is a glimpse into the future of AI integration across various aspects of life. The technology that enables a robot to compete in a fast-paced sport like table tennis has profound implications for numerous fields, from home assistance to industrial applications, where the ability of AI to learn, adapt, and cooperate with humans could lead to transformative changes.

In the realm of home assistance, the principles and technologies behind the table tennis robot can be adapted to create more capable and responsive domestic robots. Imagine a future where household robots are not just tools that perform simple tasks like vacuuming or dishwashing, but sophisticated assistants capable of understanding and anticipating the needs of the people they serve. These robots could help with everything from preparing meals to assisting with personal care, offering support that is tailored to the specific preferences and routines of the household members.

The adaptability and real-time decision-making that are key to the robot's performance in table tennis could be crucial in these domestic settings. For example, a home assistant robot could learn to recognize the daily patterns of its users—such as when they typically eat, what chores they prioritize, and how they prefer certain tasks to be done. By integrating predictive AI models, these robots could anticipate the needs of their users before they are even expressed, creating a more seamless and intuitive interaction between humans and machines.

In industrial settings, the impact of this technology could be even more significant. Robots equipped with advanced AI could work alongside human workers in factories, warehouses, and construction sites, handling tasks that require both precision and adaptability. These robots could be used to perform dangerous or physically demanding jobs, reducing the risk to human workers while increasing efficiency and productivity. By learning from human workers and adapting to the changing conditions of the workplace, these AI-driven robots could become indispensable partners in a wide range of industries.

One of the most exciting possibilities is the potential for AI to assist in environments that are too hazardous or inaccessible for humans. For instance, robots could be deployed in disaster response scenarios, where they could navigate through rubble, assess damage, and even carry out rescue operations. The same technology that allows a robot to play table tennis could be adapted to help these robots move through unpredictable and challenging terrains, making quick decisions in high-stakes situations.

The significance of AI learning to cooperate with humans cannot be overstated. In both home and industrial contexts, the ability of AI to understand and respond to human behavior is key to its successful integration into everyday life. Cooperation between humans and AI-driven machines opens up a new frontier of possibilities, where machines are not just tools but partners that can enhance human capabilities. This partnership could lead to new levels of efficiency and innovation, as AI helps to optimize processes, solve complex problems, and even inspire new ways of thinking.

As AI continues to evolve, the relationship between humans and machines is likely to become more collaborative. Rather than replacing humans, AI has the potential to augment human abilities, taking on tasks that are too complex, repetitive, or dangerous for people to handle on their own. This cooperative dynamic could lead to a future where humans and machines work together more seamlessly, each complementing the strengths of the other.

The lessons learned from the development of the table tennis robot are directly applicable to this future. The robot's ability to learn from its environment, adapt to new challenges, and cooperate with human opponents highlights the importance of flexibility and collaboration in AI design. These qualities will be essential as AI moves beyond the confines of controlled environments and into the real world, where it must navigate the complexities and unpredictability of human life.

In conclusion, the technology behind the robotic table tennis player is a harbinger of things to come. Its applications extend far beyond the sport itself, offering insights into how AI can be integrated into various aspects of life, from home assistance to industrial work.

The ability of AI to learn, adapt, and cooperate with humans will be crucial in shaping a future where machines enhance our lives in ways that were once the stuff of science fiction. As AI continues to advance, the possibilities for its integration into everyday life are virtually limitless, promising a world where humans and machines work together to achieve more than ever before.

As AI technology advances and increasingly integrates into everyday life, it brings with it a host of ethical considerations that society must grapple with. The development of AI-driven robots, such as the table tennis-playing machine, serves as a microcosm of the broader discussions surrounding the role of AI in our lives. While the potential benefits of AI are vast, ranging from enhanced efficiency to new forms of collaboration between humans and machines, there are also significant concerns that must be addressed to ensure that these technologies are developed and deployed responsibly.

One of the primary ethical considerations is the impact of AI on employment. As AI and robotics become more capable of performing tasks that were once the sole domain of humans, there is a legitimate concern that these machines could displace workers in various industries. For example, in manufacturing and logistics, where robots are already being used to perform repetitive or dangerous tasks, the fear is that as these machines become more intelligent and autonomous, they could replace human jobs on a large scale. This raises important questions about how to manage the transition to an AI-driven economy, including how to retrain workers and ensure that the benefits of AI are distributed equitably.

Another ethical concern revolves around the autonomy and decision-making capabilities of AI-driven robots. As these machines become more sophisticated, they are increasingly able to make decisions on their own, sometimes without direct human oversight. This autonomy can be beneficial, allowing robots to operate in environments where human intervention is not possible or practical. However, it also raises questions about accountability. If a robot makes a decision that leads to harm—whether it's a medical robot making a mistake during surgery or an autonomous vehicle causing an accident—who is responsible? Ensuring that there are clear guidelines and accountability mechanisms in place is crucial as AI becomes more integrated into critical areas of life.

Privacy is another significant ethical issue. AI-driven robots, especially those designed for home assistance or public spaces, often rely on extensive data collection to function effectively. This data can include personal information, behavioral patterns, and even sensitive health information. The potential for misuse of this data, whether through hacking, surveillance, or unauthorized sharing, poses a serious risk to individual privacy. Ensuring that robust safeguards are in place to protect personal data and that users have control over their information is essential to maintaining trust in AI technologies.

Beyond these specific ethical concerns, there is the broader issue of how society perceives AI-driven robots. Public perception of AI is complex and often mixed, reflecting a combination of excitement about the possibilities and apprehension about the risks. On one hand, many people are excited by the potential of AI to improve lives, increase productivity, and solve problems that were previously thought to be intractable. The idea of robots that can assist in daily tasks, enhance medical care, or even provide companionship to the elderly or those living alone is highly appealing.

However, alongside this excitement, there are also significant concerns. One of the most pervasive fears is the idea of losing control over these technologies. The notion that AI could one day surpass human intelligence and operate independently—sometimes referred to as the "AI singularity"—is a source of anxiety for many. While this scenario remains speculative, it taps into deep-seated fears about the unknown and the potential for technology to evolve beyond human understanding and control.

There is also concern about the dehumanization of society as AI becomes more prevalent. As machines take on more roles traditionally filled by humans, from customer service to caregiving, there is a fear that this could lead to a loss of personal connection and empathy in these interactions. The question of whether AI can truly understand and respond to human emotions in a meaningful way is central to this concern. While AI can simulate human-like interactions, there is a growing debate about whether these interactions can ever fully replace the nuances of human-to-human communication.

In response to these concerns, there has been a growing movement advocating for the ethical development of AI, emphasizing the importance of transparency, accountability, and inclusivity. Researchers and policymakers are increasingly recognizing the need to involve a diverse range of voices in the development of AI technologies, including ethicists, sociologists, and the general public. This inclusive approach is essential to ensuring that AI is developed in a way that aligns with societal values and addresses the concerns of all stakeholders.

In conclusion, while AI-driven robots like the table tennis player offer exciting possibilities, they also raise important ethical questions that must be carefully considered. The impact of AI on employment, autonomy, privacy, and human interaction are all areas that require thoughtful attention as these technologies continue to evolve. Public perception of AI reflects a delicate balance between hope and fear, highlighting the need for responsible development and deployment of AI systems. By addressing these ethical considerations head-on, society can better navigate the challenges of integrating AI into everyday life, ensuring that the benefits are realized while minimizing potential harms.

Conclusion

The journey of creating a robotic table tennis player, as explored throughout this book, represents both a remarkable achievement and a testament to the challenges that lie ahead in the field of AI and robotics. From the initial conception of using AI to master a physical sport, to the intricate process of training the robot through simulations and real-world practice, this endeavor has highlighted the incredible progress that has been made in bridging the gap between digital algorithms and tangible, physical actions.

The robot's ability to compete against human players, winning a significant portion of matches, underscores the advances in AI's capacity to understand, predict, and execute complex tasks. It has demonstrated strengths in speed, precision, and strategic thinking, areas where AI is beginning to rival human abilities. However, the journey has also revealed critical challenges, particularly in dealing with the nuanced aspects of human play—such as extreme spins, fast-paced rallies, and the subtle art of serving. These limitations serve as important reminders that, while AI has made impressive strides, there is still much work to be done to reach the level of human dexterity and adaptability.

Reflecting on the broader implications, this project is more than just a step forward in robotics; it is a glimpse into the future of AI's integration into various aspects of life. The technology that powers this robotic athlete has the potential to revolutionize industries far beyond sports. From home assistance to industrial automation, and from healthcare to disaster response, the principles and advancements developed here will likely be applied to a wide array of real-world challenges. The future possibilities are vast, and the ongoing journey of AI will undoubtedly continue to push the boundaries of what machines can achieve.

As we look ahead, the next steps for AI in physical tasks will involve refining predictive models, improving algorithms, and enhancing the synergy between hardware and software. These advancements will allow AI to handle more complex and dynamic environments, bringing us closer to a world where robots are not just tools but active participants in our daily lives. Whether it's through aiding in difficult tasks, working alongside humans in cooperative settings, or even participating in new forms of entertainment and sports, the role of AI in the real world is set to expand significantly.

In closing, I encourage you, the reader, to consider the broader impact of these advancements. The development of AI-driven robots raises profound questions about the future of human-machine interaction, the ethical implications of increasingly autonomous systems, and the potential for these technologies to shape our world in ways we have yet to fully imagine. As we continue to explore and develop AI, it is essential to engage in thoughtful reflection on how these technologies can be harnessed to enhance human life, while also addressing the challenges and concerns that accompany such rapid innovation.

The journey of this robotic athlete is just one chapter in the ongoing story of AI and robotics—a story that is still unfolding, full of promise, and ripe with possibilities. The future of AI is not just about machines learning to play games; it's about discovering new ways for machines and humans to collaborate, innovate, and improve the world together.

www.ingramcontent.com/pod-product-compliance
Lightning Source LLC
LaVergne TN
LVHW051616050326
832903LV00033B/4527